DILEMMAS OF THE ANGELS

DILEMMAS OF THE ANGELS

⇒ POEMS ⇐

DAVID ROMTVEDT

Louisiana State University Press Baton Rouge

Published by Louisiana State University Press
Copyright © 2017 by David Romtvedt
All rights reserved
Manufactured in the United States of America
LSU Press Paperback Original
First printing

Designer: Michelle A. Neustrom
Typeface: Newslab
Printer and binder: LSI

Library of Congress Cataloging-in-Publication Data

Names: Romtvedt, David, author.
Title: Dilemmas of the angels : poems / David Romtvedt.
Description: Baton Rouge : Louisiana State University Press, [2017]
Identifiers: LCCN 2016027487| ISBN 978-0-8071-6580-5 (pbk.
  : alk. paper) | ISBN 978-0-8071-6581-2 (pdf) | ISBN 978-0-
  8071-6582-9 (epub) | ISBN 978-0-8071-6583-6 (mobi)
Classification: LCC PS3568.O5655 A6 2017 | DDC 811/.54—dc23
  LC record available at https://lccn.loc.gov/2016027487

for
Alyson Hagy

and
in memory of
Jane Sarmiento Schwab

CONTENTS

ACKNOWLEDGMENTS

Thank you to the publications where these poems, some in different versions, appeared:

American Poetry Review: "The Phone Rings"; basalt: "Dilemmas of the Angels: The Best"; BigCityLit: "Surprise Breakfast"; Caduceus: "Dilemmas of the Angels: Reincarnation"; Cloudbank: "Camping Alone"; Monarch Review: "Progress" and "To Kisangani"; Mountain Gazette: "Sunday Morning Early"; New Works Review: "Dilemmas of the Angels: Hoping for a Snack"; North American Review: "First Communion Dress" (as "Burning My First Communion Dress"); Open Window Review: "Dilemmas of the Angels: Mojada," "My Icarus" and "Returning Home in Winter"; Paddlefish: "Dilemmas of the Angels: Change" (as "Dilemmas of the Angels: Surgery"); Pilgrimage: "Falling Asleep" and "One-Legged Dancer" (as "The War Zone"); Ploughshares: "Cheap Fiction"; Poetry East: "Adventure"; Rattle: "On Broadway," "Dilemmas of the Angels: Extraterrestrial," and "Dilemmas of the Angels: Intention"; The Same: "Coffee in Bujumbura," "Dilemmas of the Angels: Individuation," "Mojados en la frontera entre Sonora y Arizona," and "Sunday Drive"; The Sun: "To Heaven" (as "Be Actual") and "Sunday Morning Early"; Turning Wheel: The Journal of Socially Engaged Buddhism: "Submission"; Voicings from the High Country: "The Age of Risk," "Artificial Breeze," and "Losing Our Marbles."

"Still in Love" appeared in Blood, Water, Wind, and Stone: An Anthology of Wyoming Writers, edited by Lori Howe.

"Birds Singing for Jesus," "Dilemmas of the Angels: Flight," "First Time," "In Bed," and "Taking Leave" (as "Saving Me") originally appeared in Narrative magazine.

"Accident," "Illegal Alien," and "Western Aid" appeared in *An Endless Skyway: Poetry from the State Poets Laureate of America*, edited by Caryn Mirriam-Goldberg.

"Artificial Breeze" appeared in *New Poets of the American West*, edited by Lowell Jaeger.

"Losing Our Marbles" appeared in *Red Thread Gold Thread: The Poet's Voice*, edited by Alan Cohen and published to benefit the Power of Poetry Festival in Logan, Ohio.

"With Caitlin, Age 8, Building a Quinzee for a Winter Night" appeared in *Poets on Place: Interviews and Tales from the Road*, edited by W. T. Pfefferle.

"Housework" appeared in *Time and Space*, edited by Ronda Miller.

"Birds Singing For Jesus," "Dancing in Zaïre," and "Football Field, Butare, Rwanda, 1977" appeared in *A Democracy of Poets*, edited by Kim Nuzzo, Marjorie DeLuca, Cameron Scott, and Rett Harper.

"*Dilemmas of the Angels: Intention*" appeared in *Veils, Halos, and Shackles*, edited by Charles Fishman and Smita Sahay.

"Late Winter Ski Trip," "Sunday Morning Early," and "Surprise Breakfast" were broadcast on Wyoming Public Radio's *Open Spaces* program.

"Sunday Morning Early" is included in the Worthington (Ohio) Public Library's Garden Poetry Path public art project.

Thank you to my wife, Margo Brown, and daughter, Caitlin Belem Brown Romtvedt, for their love and support. Thanks also to Mark Jenkins, John Lane, Ron Manheimer, Bob Southard, Jane Sarmiento Schwab, Floyd Skloot, John Van Buren, and Terry Tempest Williams for their friendship and for the help they have given me in writing these poems. The University of Wyoming Departments of English and Creative Writing gave me a home in which I could grow as both teacher and writer. Finally, I'm grateful to Alyson

Hagy, friend and colleague at the University of Wyoming, and to Michael Wiegers, editor at Copper Canyon Press. Each was kind enough to read various drafts of the poems and offer deeply insightful comments.

Dedications are to: Margo Brown ("Returning Home in Winter"), Mark Doty ("To Heaven"), Ted Kooser ("*Dilemmas of the Angels: Desire*"), The Honorable Justice Hank Maddison ("Illegal Alien"), Caitlin Belem Brown Romtvedt ("Sunday Morning Early"), Jane Sarmiento Schwab ("Still in Love"), Connie Wieneke ("First Communion Dress"), and Laura Young ("The Phone Rings").

DILEMMAS OF THE ANGELS

Sunday Morning Early

My daughter and I paddle red kayaks
across the lake. Pulling hard,
we slip easily through the water.
Far from either shore, it hits me
that my daughter is a young woman
and suddenly everything is a metaphor
for how short a time we are granted:

the red boats on the blue-black water,
the russet and gold of late summer's grasses,
the empty sky. We stop and listen to the stillness.
I say, "It's Sunday, and here we are
in the church of the out of doors,"
then wish I'd kept quiet. That's the trick in life—
learning to leave well enough alone.

Our boats drift to where the chirring
of grasshoppers reaches us from the rocky hills.
A clap of thunder. I want to say something truer
than *I love you*. I want my daughter to know that,
through her, I live a life that was closed to me.
I paddle up, lean out, and touch her hand.
I start to speak then stop.

Taking Leave

They no longer come to my door but I see them on the street,
those young men who travel together in black slacks
and white shirts, name tags announcing them as elders.

I watch them pass on their bicycles,
also black, with backpack straps flapping,
wings working hard but too small.

This morning I found two robins—nestlings who leapt
too soon and fell or were dragged from their home—
nearly featherless with ants in their empty eyes

so that as the bicycles disappear down the street,
I grow younger and younger, a child on tiptoe
waving at those who go before me into the world.

Returning Home in Winter

I open the door as my wife steps
from the bath into the cold air,
goose bumps on her skin.
She wraps a towel around herself,
sees me watching, and unwraps it.
When she smiles, her breath rises.

The shadow of the bamboo sweeps
across the steps without stirring
the dusting of snow and we leave
no tracks as we climb the stairs
and fall into bed. The blackbird too
has a shadow. It crosses the sky
on winter afternoons, the sharp light
in the icicles hanging from the eaves.

In the lower corner of the old Chinese paintings,
a hermit or wandering monk sits at the base
of a mountain, his long hair dirty and his clothes torn.
Before him, the leafless branches of the trees wave.

Such a painting hangs near the stove
where my wife, now dressed,
sits brushing her hair.
I add wood to the fire.

Dilemmas of the Angels: Flight

Before the angel there was something else—
not this coffee shop next to a drug rehabilitation center
filled with war veterans of the past, men and women
strapped to their chairs, birds straining to rise
from piles of feathers, bones, and blood.

Drenched in sweat and a little shaky
from too much caffeine, she takes flight,
a shining white-winged trumpeter swan
crossing open water, steam rising
from the feathers' barbs. Below her,
a cormorant, unfolding its black wings,
explodes from the surface, and even fish,
leaping from the oily sheen, glide
for a moment, gills pumping
in the poisonous atmosphere.

Such longing. How large
the muscles in our shoulders must be
to lift our wings even a single time.

Birds Singing for Jesus

Jesus was a carpenter,
but it's hard to picture him
hiding nails—mornings at work,
then sharing a sandwich, a coarse joke,
later walking to the olive grove
to take a leak.

He was also a preacher
whose gaze and cool tone
made his listeners long to touch him.
But he was so famously indifferent to sex
that it seems pornographic to picture him
in bed with a wife, his leg thrown over hers,
much less an erection.

It's easier to speak of the bitter fruit
of paternity, that crown of thorns.
And what would it feel like to be the one
human only half born of humanity?

When Jesus hung on the cross,
there was little for the Roman guards to do.
They put down their spears and pulled off
their helmets. They cut slivers of wood
to clean their teeth, pitched coins at a rock
and bet on which would land closest,
kicked a wad of rags around in the dust
and, lifting their arms above their heads,
yelled, "Goal!" At sunset, they lowered
the dead man to earth.

Here we are then—strange and ordinary—
climbing down from our crosses
to drive trucks or repair TVs,
to cut meat or harvest soybeans.

Today I got a letter from my father
who died in 1950, two weeks
before I was born. The postman
explained nothing. My father said
his greatest regret was
that we would never meet.

He'd already started writing
when a nurse said, "The rain's stopped.
Wouldn't you like to look out the window?"
She propped him up with pillows and he saw
the sun on the metal surfaces of the cars,
on the galvanized blades of the rooftop ventilators,
and on a puddle where a flock of sparrows
was bathing. They flapped their wings
and the water flew up, refracting the light.
"Those birds," he wrote, "were singing away
like they were giving a concert
even if I was the only person who'd come."

There's no letter. I was an adult
when my father died an unhappy
not quite old man. He was a carpenter,
but I don't believe he could have worked on a crew
with Jesus. He could hardly work with anyone.
Still, I wanted to have another chance.
I wanted those birds to be singing for him.

On Broadway

On my ninth birthday, I was his reluctant partner.
We wore white shirts, red jackets, and black patent
leather shoes he'd bought at the Salvation Army
along with paper top hats from the party supply store
and canes made from PVC tubing he'd painted gold.
Our big number was "Putting on the Ritz."

Finished, we sat in aluminum lawn chairs
and watched the clouds cross the sky.
He whistled show tunes and told me
how to get the right inflexion to impress
a casting director. My mother came out
of the kitchen carrying drinks
and strawberries with whipped cream.

She looked at him and said, "If you worked
hard, you could still audition." Wiping his mouth
with his napkin and casually setting his plate
down for the cat, he said, "Oh, I don't know.
I can't give up the lumberyard." Then to me,
"Let's do it again, kiddo."

Relieved he hadn't thrown the plate, I exhaled,
only then aware I'd been holding my breath,
seeing for the first time his fear.

When the song ended, we tapped the edges
of our paper top hats with our PVC canes
and bowed and everyone clapped like mad,
my mother most of all.

Surprise Breakfast

One winter morning I get up early
to clean the ash from the grate
and find my daughter, eight, in the kitchen
thumping around pretending she has a peg leg

while also breaking eggs into a bowl—
separating yolks and whites, mixing oil
and milk. Her hands are smooth,
not from lack of labor but youth.

She's making pancakes for me, a surprise
I have accidentally ruined. "You never
get up early," she says, measuring
the baking powder, beating the egg whites.

It's true. When I wake, I roll to the side
and pull the covers over my head.
"It was too cold to sleep," I say.
"I thought I'd get the kitchen warm."

Aside from the scraping of the small flat shovel
on the iron grate, and the wooden spoon turning
in the bowl, the room is quiet. I lift the gray ash
and lay it carefully into a bucket to take outside.

"How'd you lose your leg?" I ask.
"At sea. I fell overboard in a storm
and a shark attacked me, but I'm fine."
She spins, a little batter flying from the spoon.

I can hear the popping of the oil in the pan.
"Are you ready?" she asks, thumping to the stove.
Fork in hand, I sit down, hoping that yes,
I am ready, or nearly so, or one day will be.

Dilemmas of the Angels: Reincarnation

Her body's a half-liter water bottle full of shredded paper,
her wings crushed soda cans—mismatched Coca-Cola
and Fanta Orange. Her head's the molded plastic head
of a doll over which hovers her halo—the tin lid
of a frozen juice container. Her mouth turns up
in a quizzical smile as if she might be
the Mona Lisa, face paralyzed.

You'd think an angel would be a big deal.
Instead, there's an angel for every little thing.
When one disappears another comes into being.

This one stands in a Styrofoam crèche stained
purple to match her hair. There are curtains
made from the mesh bags that hold lettuce
in the produce section of the supermarket.
Maybe the curtains make it a theater not a crèche.
Atop everything is a Styrofoam arch, a bigger halo
out of which rise sixteen burnt wooden matches.

She steps from the crèche and nearly falls.
There's a switch glued to her back off-center
so she's heavier on one side than the other.
It makes her walk with a hitch. She has to
concentrate to pick up a plastic hubcap
meant to approximate chrome. Somewhere
in the grass there's a child's tiara, a crown
with which she might come back a queen.
What about a scepter? Maybe the antenna
snapped off a pickup or the wind-blasted
leg bone of an elk. She drops the hubcap
and walks on, the hitch giving her a sexy
look, the suggestion of another life.

Dancing in Zaïre

Hot afternoons we swam across the lake
and walked home along the shore, stopping
in town at the music shop. On the counter
ten portable turntables were going at once.
When somebody left, you jumped forward
and asked for Lipua Lipua or Dr. Nico
or l'Orchestre African Fiesta and the man
who ran the shop took the 45 rpm record
from its sleeve, touching only the edges,
and handed it to you, and by the time
somebody finally bought a record,
it'd have a million scratches.

Near sunset, we walked to the market
where the old women sat on mats selling
paper pyramids of roasted groundnuts
and ten kilo bags of rice filled with rocks.
The old men drank in the still hot shade
of the pavilion's corrugated metal roof—
banana and sorghum beer sucked through
long straws from fifty-five gallon drums.
We stood and talked about l'authenticité.

It felt good and we forgot we were speaking
French and not Kiswahili, Lingala, or Tshiluba.
President Mobutu outlawed ties and jackets
as signs of European bondage, and renamed
our country Zaïre and the river Zaïre and even
the money Zaïre. No one was called madame
or monsieur. We were citoyen and citoyenne.
It was beautiful to be equal.

We picked new names. Joseph-Désiré Mobutu
became Mobutu Sese Seko Nkuka Ngbendu
wa Za Banga—the all powerful warrior who
because of his endurance and indefatigable
will to win goes from conquest to conquest
leaving fire in his wake. It was exciting
to think we might be free.

Maybe it's not fair to say it ended up as bad
as before. We went to Mobutu's compound
and, hiding from the soldiers, climbed the fence.
We could see the flowers and trees, the fruit
fallen to the ground, uneaten. They said
Mobutu had elephants but I don't know.

Where we lived there were only monkeys
screeching in the trees. It wasn't so hot
and it was too high for tsetse flies
so no sleeping sickness though we had malaria.
All through the rainy season, we made fires
to drive away the mosquitoes. I loved the smoke
and mist, the sweet smell of burning garbage
and eucalyptus leaves, and dancing at night
in leaking pavilions to the scratched records
someone had bought in the shop.

Western Aid

We worked in the East African hill country
running a parasite dipping tank. Local farmers
brought their cows and goats twice a week
and the animals were led into an ever narrowing chute
until they were forced to walk single file
to the lip of a concrete tank filled with pesticide.
They balked and bellowed, and tried to turn.
Their feet slipped out from under them
on the oozing carpet of urine and excrement
left by those who'd gone ahead.

Finally, they fell into the pesticide-laden water
and swam for their lives. At the far side of the tank
the bottom sloped up and the terrified animals
stumbled back onto land where they shook
and ran then stopped to lick themselves.

One morning a patrol appeared. The soldiers
had removed the mirrors from the front fenders
of their Jeep and, on the vertical steel supports,
had mounted the heads of captured rebels
they were fond of calling communists.

"Vous n'en avez pas?" Ambiguous,
the question might have pertained
to medicines, gasoline, canned milk,
or rebels disguised as starving farmers.
"Nous ne cachons rien," my coworker said.
"We are hiding nothing," then pointed at the heads
and added, "c'est pas juste." "It's not right."

The Jeep driver stepped forward
and poked the barrel of his rifle
into her chest. I heard the quick
inhalation as he flipped the weapon
and then, swinging it two-handed
like a tennis player from another era,
knocked her down. When she didn't rise,
he moved to strike her again. A second
soldier held him back and they left,
heads wobbling on their mounts.

Dilemmas of the Angels: Koans

In Zen they ask questions
that have no answers. They ask
how to enter through a gateless gate
or what was my original face, or yours,
or does a dog have Buddha nature.
Of course a dog has Buddha nature,
she thinks without thinking,
then wonders.

The most famous koan is about
the sound of one hand clapping.

In Japan, they sell koan answer books.
In America, such books are available
in translation. Still, even after reading
the book again and again, the answer
may be right or wrong.

She's practicing harp. It's hard
with so many strings so close together.
If she makes a mistake, the sound
of the wrong note will go on forever.
It's like a stone dropped in a pond
and the waves go out in circles
till they reach the shore. Only
there is no shore. Nervous, she
stops practicing and, in the silence,
hears a dog barking up a storm.

One-Legged Dancer

Here in the war zone, the dance hall
stays open. When the bombs explode,
lights flicker and dust hovers in the air,
couples flail then grab one another.

The security guards watch the dancers
jerk and heave. Their gaze is the same
as that directed by soldiers at insurgents
breaking up asphalt to bury roadside bombs.

At a table in a darkened corner a man sits alone.
He lost a leg to a land mine and can't walk
but when the next song starts, he stands. Without
a partner, he turns his head and lifts his arms.

The security guards go on watching as the man
steadies himself to hop on one leg. He snaps
his fingers. Sweat falls from his face and the sound
of his breathing, as in sex, implies both pleasure and pain.

Outside, the insurgents and soldiers are still at it
There's an explosion and the sound of breaking glass.
The man closes his eyes and his hands slide down
along the curve of his invisible partner's back.

When a second explosion rocks the building,
the man loses his balance. Still, the security guards
watch and no one rushes forward, no matter
the longing, no one moves to help.

Football Field, Butare, Rwanda, 1977

1.

The white man ascends the platform
with the foreign friends of the nation,
another umuzungu in line to meet
President Habyarimana Juvenal.
Though he's been told not to,
he looks into the president's eyes,
the flecks of gold swimming
in the whites. Juvenal gazes
to the other end of the field
where the Intore Dancers hammer
the ground with their bare feet,
the dusty jingling rising from bells
tied to their ankles and calves.
Still not looking at him, Juvenal
takes the umuzungu's hand, holds it
a little too tightly, a little too long,
says "Les amis du pays."

2.

The white man plays softball
with the *Québécois coopérants
étrangers*, shirts and hats for bases.
A long fly to center and he backs up
across the field to the bleachers
built by German colonialists
before the world gave Rwanda
to the Belgians. He clambers up
three rows, arms outstretched.
The ball falls into his glove
like the first flake of snow falling
onto his tongue when he was a child.
The players whistle and cheer

and the shortstop runs to him,
thumps him on the back and shouts,
"Mais ça, ça c'est bon, ça."
A really good catch.

3.

The white man falls in love
with a local woman. They walk
to a cinder block bar with a tin roof
and drink Primus in liter bottles.
The barman's twelve-year-old daughter
plays the same six soukous records
over and over, the polyrhythmic songs
spinning the dancers into two worlds.
The woman touches the man's waist,
says, "Tu vois, non?" Hip like this,
shoulder here. The floor is littered
with peanut shells and happiness,
and the laughter in the room is as warm
as the beer in its sweating bottle.
When the moon goes down,
the man and woman walk to the field.
In the open expanse where no one sees,
they lie in the dust and make love
as if history never happened.

Dilemmas of the Angels: Desire

Krishna tells her that if she desires
with all her heart, she will get what she wants.
He neglects to mention what she must give up.

Like many people she's visited the museum
at Auschwitz where the bodies were stacked.
People say like shoes or firewood.

She could undo the Holocaust,
give life back
to the prematurely dead.

She is only an angel, a fly
in the mind of God, infinitely giddy
from the ease of her escape.

Her desire has about as much weight
as a beauty contestant's longing for world peace,
her dress backless to show off her wings.

Krishna explains that he is a man
whose stage-four cancer makes him ultrasensitive
to light so that he can go outside only at night.

When he smiles, the skin tightens on his skull
as if to say it is brevity that fans the fire of desire,
and brevity that is the fire's consummation.

To Kisangani

The travelers push upriver for a week,
the wood-fired boiler steaming.

Animal cages stacked on deck, rust flaking
from the rail, the opaque water churning.

In Tanzania they saw flamingos at Makat,
lake of salt, the pale feathers, pink blood.

And in Rwanda, the church with its pews
ruined under a rain of machete blows.

The road curves along the river, the city
leaning backward as if it might slip away.

The charcoal makers shake ash into the sky,
foreign shopkeepers smoking in doorways.

A dark lump bumps the hull—a rotting hemp sack
or an unidentifiable dead animal or who knows.

The boat grinds back into the current, monkeys
screaming and throwing feces from the trees.

Coffee in Bujumbura

When we felt done in by life in Rwanda,
we'd hitch a ride to Bujumbura and pretend
we'd gone to Europe. The Greek refugees
left from World War II had started restaurants
and put tables on the shattered sidewalks
with umbrellas and flower boxes and music
piped through electric speakers out of doors.

You could order baklava and espresso
in porcelain cups, sugar and, if you asked,
canned milk. The waiter smiled and the clouds
looked happy crossing the sky unconcerned
about where they went or who was following them.
Even so, when we lifted the cups to our mouths,
though the coffee was good, it was hard to drink.

Dilemmas of the Angels: Individuation

In front of the mirror the angel tries on
outfit after outfit. Not that she has so many
but if you wear the same clothes to school
two days in a row, you never hear the end of it.

This week she learned the word *individuation*.
"A good word," her teacher said, "though
it should be avoided for reasons of style."

First, there was unity, then thinking was separated
from thinker. How did that happen? The Lord sprung
from his own loins? The fall was not Adam and Eve
eating of the tree of the knowledge of good and evil
but the Lord creating the tree in the first place.
If you want Heaven, you have to have Hell.

It occurs to her that the man she has known
as her Lord and Savior is no enlightened being.
She wants to take him by the shoulders, shake him
and shout, "Wake up! Look what you've done!"
There she is, alone in bed, shaking the air,
tears falling from her cheeks, the clock ticking
on the nightstand, her head pounding.

She stumbles to the bathroom for aspirin
and, opening the medicine cabinet, remembers
that no one can enter Heaven alone. She swallows
the aspirin without water, walks back to bed,
and lies there trying not to think. The walls surround her.
To the unaided eye, they look motionless. But they're breathing,
long slow breaths, so generous they can't be seen.

With Caitlin, Age 8, Building a Quinzee for a Winter Night

In the morning we shovel snow into a mound
six feet high and fifteen feet across, then push
twelve-inch-long twigs into the mound.
In the afternoon we dig, shaping a doorway
and hollowing out a room. When snow blocks
the door, we work in darkness on our backs,
shoveling until we break through to light.
Finally, we sit up to shape the ceiling.
When the twigs come into view, we stop.

We lay out ground pads and sleeping bags,
set a candle in a spoon and push the handle
into the domed wall of snow. By candlelight
we read aloud *The Chronicles of Narnia*.
Though the book's children must fight evil
to bring back summer, we don't care.
The burnished light from the candle dances
on both the snow walls and our faces.
We are warm in our sleeping bags.
When my daughter falls asleep,
I sleep, too.

In the night I wake up, needing to pee.
I wriggle out of my bag and slide on my back
through the doorway, the cold hammering
my face. The blue-black sky comes into view
then the stars and, finally, the moon.

I stick my head back in and wake my daughter.
"You have to see this. Lie on your back and look up
when you come out." As her face emerges, she blinks
and her mouth opens. She says the single word, "Oh."

We stand, hold hands, and jump around
watching the thermometer on my coat, waiting
for it to adjust—26 below. We slide back in
on our stomachs, crawl into our sleeping bags,
and read a few more pages of the story.
"It was beautiful," Caitlin says. "Yes."
When she sits up to blow out the candle,
she bumps the wall and a little snow
falls onto her sleeping bag. "Careful,
you have to stay dry in the cold."

In the morning we wake, slide out
and stand once more in the frozen air,
ice crystals hovering around us, the stars
still in sight. "26 below," I say. "Not many
eight year olds have slept out in that kind of cold."
"But we built a quinzee," she reminds me.
"It's warmer in there." She throws herself down
on the snow, slapping at it, and grinning at the sky.

My Icarus

It was on a Thursday when a young man
dropped from the sky into my backyard.
I know it was Thursday because that's when
I do the gardening, which between mowing,
trimming, mulching, weeding, and watering,
takes all day. The mulch is my favorite part—
spreading the cut grass around the plants
to keep the ground cool in the desert heat.

The young man hit one of the railroad ties
I'd used to make raised beds for vegetables
and broke his elbow—the bend of his wing—
or that's what I thought but when I looked
closer I saw goose feathers glued carefully
to a hand-carved wooden armature attached
with leather belts to his shoulders and chest.

So this is Icarus. How could he be here
so far from the Pacific and farther still
from the Aegean? When he fell, his father
came swooping down to find a sheen
of white feathers on the shining black sea.

He cried out and cursed himself
for inventing human flight.
He'd given his son the same warning
my father gave me—"Don't fly too close
to the sun for the heat will melt the wax,
the feathers will fall off and you will fall."
I've fallen more times than I can count
but keep trying to fly, feeling it is my duty
to get as close to the sun as possible.
Like other young men, I ignored
my father's warnings and now
that he's dead I can't apologize.

I lifted the youth from the railroad tie
and saw that when he hit the tomatoes,
they cushioned his fall and he was smeared
not with blood but with the crushed fruit—
a mixture of too many Hollywood movies
and my aging eyes which I hate to admit
don't work as well as they once did.

I helped him to a lawn chair, gave him a beer
with lime juice, and went back to mowing.
I use an electric mower and the blue cord
trails behind, the jerky electrons turning
the blade to chew up the grass.

He coughed and set the beer aside.
Then he stood and came toward me,
pointing at the mower and waving his arms,
his cough so violent that I worried
he might hurt himself. When I touched him,
he shook off my hand and began pushing
the mower—faster and faster until his feet
barely touched the ground.

To Heaven

I'm at a friend's house. He's dying and we're
watching television. A handsome actor
comes on and my friend says, "Do you think
he could love a man who spends all day in bed?"
"You were up just yesterday," I remind him.
"To take a shit," he says. "And I couldn't do that."

For the past two months he's been writing
on the walls with a thick black marking pen.
He'll get a burst of energy and drag himself
from room to room. When I come over
he asks me to read the day's efforts aloud:
*Religion must include not only longing
and need but anger.* "Oh God," he groans.
"How could I be so boring?"

"It's not boring," I assure him.
"Even if it's crap, boring's not the issue."
"It's crap?" he asks. "Yes, it's crap."
"It's crap," he shouts, "I can still produce
crap." And smiles, happy to have
a little phony drama in place
of the real one in which he plays
the tragic leading man. I read on—
*Traveling between two worlds
I find I am mute in both.* And finally,
*What's the difference between the day
before the diagnosis and the day after?*

The writing starts at the floor and rises.
"I wasn't thinking ahead," he says.
"I've filled the low parts so that if I want
to write more I have to sit up. After that,
I'll have to stand. If I'd started at the ceiling,
I could have worked down."

"Don't worry," I say. "We'll get a foam pad
and put it on a scaffold. We can crank you up
so you can write as high as you want."
"To Heaven?" he asks.
"To Heaven."

Home again and unable to sleep,
I lay in bed thinking how short life is
and what is the best thing to do with it.
I'd never mention this to my friend,
who has grown less patient with banality.

I got up and walked around the house
then went to my desk, pulled out a marker,
and started writing on the wordless walls.

Dilemmas of the Angels: The Best

She knows where I can buy
the best non-dairy low-fat ice cream
at a reduced price, and she knows the address
of the best plumbing supply store in town.
When she presented the award for the best
fire suppression program to the Worland, Wyoming,
office of the Bureau of Land Management,
she wore a low cut gown that revealed
deep cleavage and did more than hint
at the perfection of her breasts.
Her beauty shop offers the best haircut,
manicure, and pedicure, and in surgery
she has completed the best, most painless hysterectomy.
Her acupuncture treatment cures lack of faith.
She is a part owner of the best animal grooming shop,
and is a member of the committee that picked this year's
best movie, book, recording, song, poem, and painting of the year.
She can name the best mother, father, daughter, son, husband, wife,
grandma, and grandpa, the best teacher in the district, in the state,
in the country, the best teacher in Heaven—oops, she's let slip
that even in Heaven there is best and second best.
But second best is not what interests her.

"Who is the best poet?" she asks me
and I want to smack her. "Well, then,"
she goes on with a nasty little grin,
"who is the best Latin American poet?
The best woman poet in Ohio?
The best dead poet?
The best living poet who writes like a dead poet?
The best non-Spanish speaking Chicano younger poet
living in a former French colony? Who?"

I know I've alluded to her beauty but
she has the best figure for a model over forty.
She is the best time I ever had
and your best bet for a good time, too,
the best lay, the best Catholic priest,
the best lay Catholic priest.
She's the best ride at Disney World,
the best religion,
the best in the West,
the best-handling car on the road,
and the one that gets the best mileage,
the hundred best rock songs of the twentieth century not available in
    retail stores,
the best interior lineman on a team that has never won the Super Bowl,
the best-dressed Hollywood star,
the best chance to win the presidency,
the best bullet, rocket, hand grenade, land mine,
the best prosthetic device,
the best bomb
and the best underground bomb shelter.

The angel pauses to take a breath.
That useless bomb shelter has put her in another
state of mind. She is as much Buddhist apologist
as Christian cheerleader and it hits me
we haven't even gotten to the worst,
that alluring other form of the best,
the best former angel, fallen, say, to Hell.

Adventure

I lie on the grass reading
Money and the Meaning of Life
then stop, let the book fall,
and close my eyes.
The Senior Men's soccer team
is practicing on the YMCA field.
When I open my eyes,
there's a boy raking leaves
and stuffing them into black plastic bags.
Two women walk by, sit near me,
eat their lunch, get up, and leave.
Over my right shoulder, Odysseus
slips from his boat into the sea
and it is not so much wine dark
as the pale blue of a human eye.
I stand up and walk home,
excited to see my wife,
but she's out doing errands
and has left a note asking me
about a stack of unpaid bills—
electricity, water, insurance.
I'm happy because I have
enough money to pay the bills,
happy to feel the ink beginning
to flow in my cheap ballpoint pen.

Still in Love

A small earthquake tonight, no real damage
but enough to make the ground shift
and the door, loose on its hinges, rattle.

Reading, I'd drifted off and while I'd been
chipping away at the stone of sleep,
it took the earthquake to wake me up.

I walked out into the moonless night
and tried to think about politics and justice,
but it was no go as the earth still trembled.

What about sex? While I feel less the savage
tension of the body, I still love and, as a lover,
feel both more vulnerable and more reliable.

It's hard to separate seeing from wishing. What is
this talking, these words that come from my mouth?
I'm not so much saying them as being said.

The earth has gone still and down the long valley,
some bird is calling, turning darkness to song.
It seems so romantic—this earthquake.

Losing Our Marbles

My father said it wasn't so much
getting old he feared as losing his marbles.
That would be the worst.

I listened to him tell the neighbor,
but I thought about the neighbor's son
who had a glass eye.

At school, he'd take it out and wave it at the girls,
chasing them around the playground. They screamed,
even then kind enough to pretend to be afraid.

His name was Elgin. Everybody else
was named Tony and Joe and Marcos
or Guadalupe and Linda. Elgin seemed English.

And royal. He should have been the son
of a duke or an earl
not of a long-haul truck driver.

But we lived in Arizona not England. We had no
Archbishop of Canterbury, only lice-ridden Father Kino,
whose bones were buried in the church at Magdalena—

the pilgrims on their knees
crawling toward the altar, promising
to do penance if their boons were granted.

We were on our knees, too, marbles sticky
in our sweaty palms, shaking before the shots
and what we might lose,

trying to imagine ourselves hunters
sighting down the barrels of our rifles
at rare tigers or unpredictable wild boars.

When Elgin took his eye out of its socket,
I thought he might wedge it between his thumb
and forefinger to shoot, but he leapt

and the girls ran and I don't know why,
but I thought of my father, one day older,
and all of us afraid of losing our marbles.

Dilemmas of the Angels: Change

At Mass, in the middle of the homily,
God tells her He's having a sex change.

"You never see the surgeon,"
he says, "'cause you're out cold."

"What?" "Well, you might see her
beforehand—to talk, you know."

Picturing God with pierced ears
and breasts, she smiles.

"You think I'm joking but eternity . . ."
He shrugs. "It's a long time."

Then, "Some of the angels are upset.
They don't want to work for a woman.

But times change, I change, and the Church
has to change to keep up. You understand."

"Yes," she says, "but can you really believe
a sex change means the Church is keeping up?"

Before she can say more He touches her arm,
whispers, "Not now. This is my favorite part."

First Time

When I was a boy an older boy gave me a magazine
with photos of naked women. "Keep it," he said.
In my room, I ran my fingers along the images of lips
and teeth, golden skin, and dark triangles of pubic hair.

The exposed breasts, flattened and sealed,
were enormous beneath the paper's shine.
As my pupils widened to let in more light,
there appeared inside each a still pond.

I tucked the magazine in the back of my closet
on a low shelf beneath my underwear and socks,
my freshly laundered and suddenly sweaty clothing.
One day it was gone, replaced by a Catechism book.

The years pass and bring neither warning nor advice.
I see my mother in my absence and, farther back,
see her for the first time—a young woman, her face bright
and her arms thrown forward in a gesture of welcome.

Late Winter Ski Trip

Rubbing my hands to keep warm,
I sit in the trees and watch the snow hut melt,
the rain falling like girders
from the tops of buildings.

I stare into the mist
trying to see down the mountain
to the houses below,
smoke rising from the chimneys.

My daughter and I eat breakfast—raisins and nuts
in tin cups of yogurt. She paces, now and again
looking up at the dark clouds. Under her coat her skin
is smooth with only buds where there will be breasts.

The rain turns to hail—teeth cracked
from the mouth of the sky. Finished eating
and anxious to set off, we nearly pour
the sticky red klister wax onto our skis.

Now the hail softens becoming snow,
the disembodied wings of angels falling.
There's no point in waiting any longer,
no point in staying forever in the trees.

The Age of Risk

We built a toy boat
and drilled a hole in the deck
to insert the mast. We sewed
a tiny sail and tinier flag.

Two pebbles were people,
taped down so they wouldn't fall off.
We set the boat on the surface of the pond
to watch its stately progress toward the other shore.

I see you are remembering our minor folly—
we had forgotten to tie up the dog and he lunged
into the water, snapping at the boat. Down it went,
the little sailors hauling on their lines.

We dove after them, thrashing around in the cool
green light, coming up to laugh and shout at the dog,
now barking at nothing. Had the boat reappeared,
he might have sent it again to its watery grave.

A cloud passed across the sun
and I shivered. We should have
given it a name. How much better
it is to face doom with a name.

Then the sun was back. The dog bounded
out of the water, shook, and sat next to me
watching the pond go calm, seemingly
convinced another boat was on the way.

Dilemmas of the Angels: Extraterrestrial

The aliens land and at first she's scared.
Has her Lord been keeping secrets?
Another wife and kids in a faraway galaxy?

It would be tempting. Imagine saying,
"Let there be light." And, poof, there's light.
The magic word is any word you want it to be—
Bucket, for example, or asphalt, and into the world
tumble jet planes, hair dryers, and vegetarian restaurants.

The Mayans say God made human beings from mud,
but when it rained they washed away and he had
to start over. So maybe we're the other family.

Now the aliens are stepping out of their ship,
which looks like a giant corncob painted blue.
That's a nice detail, she thinks—that blue.

Could be these people created themselves.
Certainly our Lord didn't attend so to detail.
Here it was light, dark, firmament, seas,
vault of heaven—all pretty vague. It wasn't
even clear whether angels have sexual organs.
Take that Cole Porter song—"Birds do it, bees
do it, even educated fleas do it." What about angels?

The problem is
there is no one
before whom the Lord
can bow his head
and be born again.

The aliens take off their shoes and socks
before walking barefoot across the lawn.
There's something appealing about them—
those smiles. They're taking off their clothes,
space suits really, and lying down on the grass.
They're wrapping their arms and legs around each other.
They're doing what is done to create a new being.

"Hey," she shouts, not that she's a prude,
but she's been in the garden before
and knows that the sprinklers come on
at dusk which it almost is. And what if, under
the screen of water, they are washed away?

Mojados en la frontera entre Sonora y Arizona

They stand in a line, legs spread,
arms held above their heads,

hands pressed hard into the side of the truck,
palms burning on the hot paint.

The border patrol officers in Kevlar flak jackets
sweat and pace, wipe their brows, wait.

An alien lifts his boot to scratch his leg
and an officer slaps him with a stick.

A state cruiser pulls up and parks
in the weak shade of a mesquite tree

and a large man gets out, stands for a moment,
removes his sunglasses, and turns to the fence

as if there on the other side he can see Mexico
laid out like a cow waiting to be butchered.

Another alien turns and looks down
the line of greasy levis and dusty boots

toward the sun that drops
over the distant curve of the earth.

Dilemmas of the Angels: Hoping for a Snack

She opens the refrigerator and the void looms—
no tomatoes or turkey, chocolate or chile, no corn,
no pumpkins, pineapples, peanuts or potatoes,
no avocado or nopal, no papaya. It's embarrassing—
in Cuba, some people can't say papaya out loud
without snickering—island slang for vagina.
Fruta bomba, they say, as if that's better.

She closes the door, sits down, and fingers
the locket she wears, its silver chain cool
on the skin above her breasts, the past
waiting there. On the left, a faded photo
of Che Guevara with his idealism and asthma.
On the right, Emiliano Zapata—she swoons
before his peasant good looks. Or maybe
It's only hunger that makes her faint.

On the table there's a bowl of wrinkled
grapes labeled United Farm Workers—
the black Aztec eagle on a red field.
Beside the bowl is a single bruised banana,
its blue and white United Fruit Company sticker
showing a girl wearing a plate of fruit for a hat.
Chiquita, the angel thinks, that could be me,
my head coquettishly turned, the fruit nearly
falling, smiling on behalf of those who deposed
Jacobo Arbenz for giving land to Mayan farmers.
Isn't it kings not presidents you depose?

She's suddenly dizzy like when her dad
held her by an arm and a leg and spun her round.
The fruit has to fall. And what if she throws up?
The clock ticks off the minutes. She closes the locket
and drops it inside her dress, leans forward and again
opens the refrigerator, hoping only for a snack.

41

Illegal Alien

When I was drafted to fight in Vietnam,
my father, who was in the Army Air Corps
during World War II and twice shot out of the sky,
who spent a year in hospital undergoing plastic surgery
and attempted suicide, told me, "It doesn't matter
if your country is right or wrong,
when you are called to fight, you go."

Afraid, I told my roommate, who was Canadian.
He told his father, who called me and said,
"You're not a coward for refusing to become a killer,"
then offered me a job. And so I began my new life
in British Columbia, an illegal alien on a landscape
garden crew. I mowed lawns, dug in mulch,
planted bushes, fertilized flowers, trimmed trees,
and drank beer. Each day I was paid in cash.

When the war ended, I came home and now
I'm a respectable American reading about the fence
being built along the southern border of the nation—
Texas, New Mexico, Arizona, California,
a fence from sea to shining sea to keep out Mexicans
and Guatemalans, Salvadorans and Colombians,
to keep out *la gente humilde, la gente sin medios.*
Even the shadows will find no access
to move across the ground.

These days I drive long distances to work
and return late to the sage grasslands
and pine forest, to the creek, the tumble of water
I can hear from my bedroom window,
the dark mountains rising near my house,
far from any border.

Sometimes in the night when I can't sleep,
I turn on the radio and listen to mysteries
from the Golden Age of Broadcasting,
exhortations of evangelical Christians,
Omaha grain market reports, and political
commentators shouting down their guests.
When it's late and the air is still, I hear
a faint voice from British Columbia in French.
"Et maintenant," the announcer says,
"pour la région du Delta, le météo."
It starts to rain and I remember
the sparkling lawns and blooming flowers,
the weather report then the cheery wish
that I have a good evening—
"Nous vous souhaitons une bonne nuit"—
and the sign off—"Toujours
de Vancouver, Ici Radio Canada."

Dilemmas of the Angels: Mojada

She's reading. Not that she hauled a book
to this spot west of Nogales where she waits
to cross the border into Arizona. It was on the chair
where the *pollero* left her. *Pollero*—chicken keeper.
When she was a child, they called the men who took
the poor across *coyotes*. That rang of romance.
Not this—a chicken in the jaws of a coyote, a chicken
in a cage, a chicken in a stew. She drops the book
to the floor and closes her eyes—her father paralyzed
by a stroke and her mother caring for him.

She fingers the stub of her first ticket—
not valid for passage, just a receipt,
and not to Tijuana—it's too dangerous—
nor to Juarez—that's worse. Maybe here
where the hills roll to the north
and at the fence keep rolling,
the grasses waving in the wind.

The night and the book are equally long
and maybe that is a kind of luck. The moon
crosses the sky without a sound, going down
midway between dusk and dawn. The *pollero*
arrives with wigs, false eyelashes, stockings,
pants, and shirts. "*Soy Virgilio,*" he says.
"Stuff your wings into your coat. *¡Apúrate!*"
He hands her a Phoenix to Nogales and return
bus ticket with the first half used as if she had
gone for a weekend to walk among the stalls—
the pint bottles of vanilla and cheap guitars,
the straw hats with *Mexico Alegre* on the crown.
He also gives her an Arizona driver's license
with her picture and name—Beatriz de la Garza.
A heron flies down a river course, folding its wings
to land in the shallows and wait on stick legs for a fish.

44

She holds the book up and opens her mouth.
"Yes," the *pollero* says, "I know, I take names
where I find them. Last week it was Doroteo and Paco—
Dorothy and Frank en *inglés*—from *The Wizard of Oz*.
I take you across. Once you're in Phoenix,
you're on your own. Leave the book."

At the fence under the glare of night-spotting lights,
she is surrounded by dogs, helicopters, border patrols,
saguaro cactus, hunger, thirst, and now, as she waits
to enter the traffic in undocumented souls, fear.

The dust rises and the night grows hotter. If only
she could stay home and read to her father, kiss
her mother, and go to bed where she'd turn out
the light and, again, let the book drop to the floor,
and it would mean nothing more than that.

Cheap Fiction

I'd read the book before,
but when the building blew up I found myself
drawn in again. I knew the wife would yell, "Oh,"
as her husband fell. There would be the darkness
of night and the way the world becomes a gray swirl
before our eyes. I picked up a section of orange
that lay on a plate beside me and ate.
The cat began to purr, pulling at my pant leg.

When the mail came, there was a letter from my mother.
"I couldn't tell you or your sister," she wrote, "the relief
I felt when your father died." Then my uncle called,
said, "I never liked your father. He ruined my sister's life.
But he was a man who could work, I'll give him that.
And you're the same—of all my nephews you're the one
who's not afraid to put your hands in shit and blood
if that's what it takes. Anyway, I'm sorry." "Thanks,"
I said, putting another slice of orange into my mouth.

I read on, ignoring the wars, the storms and fires,
the drone strike gone wrong in a quiet neighborhood.
I wondered about the rare flowering trees, the smell
of dust after rain, the family dog who'd disappeared.

My uncle was wrong. I was afraid. Like my mother
who couldn't admit relief, I couldn't admit longing
for my father's death. For years he'd terrorized me—
screaming, landing blows that would blast to pieces
the silence he claimed was his. Another building
blown up leaving behind only words. Surely words
might bring understanding, I thought, still greedy
for the orange and the book.

Accident

My father rises from the asphalt
and turns, his look of alarm
preceding the pain.

He was working on the loading dock
when the tractor trailer fell, the hitch
landing on his arms and breaking the bones.

With the worker's comp money, he bought me
a piano accordion. "Good easy work," he said.
"Keep your ass off a loading dock."

For a year his arms were encased in heavy casts
held up with metal armatures, his hands suspended
away from his body, useless as windows in a coffin.

At mealtime I lifted the spoon to his open mouth,
his eyes drilling into mine. "I gave my arms for you,"
he said between bites. "I gave my arms."

I was nervous. He'd hit me plenty before the accident
or the accordion. What if he turned his head
and I missed, and the food dribbled down his chin?

One day it happened. Not that I missed,
but in the middle of lunch, for no reason I knew,
he lunged, knocking me out of my chair.

Before hitting the floor, I could see it in the past—
the funny way memory, even of a painful event,
becomes a pleasure—the midday sun in the bright kitchen,

my father rising as if he might fly, his bent arms
wrapped in plaster giving him the look of an angel
with petrified wings, a blur of white swinging toward me.

Orientation

"Three things," he says, "gamma globulin,
anti-malaria prophylaxis, and soldiers.
Don't offer one a drink. Don't smile.
Don't make eye contact. Unpredictable.
Oh, yeah, clean drinking water. Four things."

In the bar one blocks the door
while the other approaches my table.
Head down, I finger the foreign national
identity card in my pocket—*Ami de le Pays*—
Friend of the Nation—my name written
on a typewriter that had a broken R.

Rifle slung across his shoulder,
he's got a liter of Primus, bottle
sweating in the heat, and two glasses,
greasy where they've been pinched
between thumb and forefinger.

I look up and see my father coming
toward me. He sets the glasses down
and starts to pour. I shake my head.
It's Rwanda not my childhood kitchen.

"Assiez-vous," I say and lift my glass,
wave at a chair, at the soldier in the door,
at another chair. "Assiez-vous," again.
Unpredictable. And drink.

Dilemmas of the Angels: A Tip

Dressed in blue sequins and red gloves, her eyes
ringed with dark powder and her lips coated
with bronze gel, she paces with the multitude
until, tired, she stops and leans on a parking meter.
A former man wearing hot pants and a blond wig,
offers her a cigarette, a light, and a tip.

"Look at these bitches massaging themselves
in public for a nickel bag," the former man says.
"Night Flyers—you don't want to end up like that."
And grinds the stub of her cigarette under her heel.

"No, not like that," the angel says, wondering
about the former man, forgetting her own cigarette
burning down until she leaps, feeling the flame.

"Some night you wake up under an abandoned
Ford Galaxy outside a stranger's apartment.
And there's no point waiting for Mr. Right
to come walking down the street in a fine suit
'cause it ain't gonna happen. Just a tip."

"It ain't gonna happen," the angel repeats,
dragging herself out from under the car.
But before she can walk away, some
invisible soul pins her arms to her sides
and slams her into the dumpster behind
the liquor store. "Jesus," the former man
says, "are you even listening?"

Progress

In the bay at Mombasa, a man swims
through the dark rainbows, the oil
leaking from tankers rocking at anchor.

He brushes against a steel hull, comes away
smeared with the smell. The wind picks up
and in the chop of waves he chokes, swallows
a mouthful of thickened water, almost sweet.

Though the air is cool, there's the usual swarming
of flies and mosquitos, the strutting of black-and-white
crows along the shore. He paddles on his back looking up.

How easy it is—arms rising in a circle
from his waist and over his face.
He can't see his hands ahead of him,
how they pull him backward.

Dilemmas of the Angels: The Garden

Since he evicted Adam and Eve,
nobody much uses the Garden.
There's a padlock on the gate
and a NO TRESPASSING sign
in seven thousand languages.

In the cool of the evening,
she hikes up her skirt
and climbs the fence.

The perennial hedges have run wild
and the annual flowers have gone to hell.
Still, it's beautiful—the butterscotch smell
of ponderosa pine next to the dry rattle
of palm fronds as if to say anything is possible.

That's when she sees him
there by the oleander playing solitaire
and drinking coffee. Could he really
have meant they'd never come home?

He lifts his cup and turns to her.
The look in his eyes—she can't breathe.
Somehow, before he speaks, she spreads
her wings and flies, leaving behind a trail
of stars, tears lighting the dark sky.

Artificial Breeze

I walked up and down the field
while my sister stood on the trailer,
the mountains in the distance.

The plains were dry and hot.
We were loading hay. Without a hook,
I lifted each bale by hand—forty pounds—
the plastic cord cutting into my gloves.

Her feet spread and her knees bent,
she grabbed the bales and shoved them
like bricks crisscrossing so that though
they rose above the cab of the truck,
they didn't fall. We went on wordlessly
under the rumble of the engine,
the thump of the bales on the flatbed
boards then on each other. Sweat
dripped from my eyelids. Sweat
ran down my chest and back.

"What a load of shit," she said, she
who has done this work so many years.
Once it was mine, too, but now—
good luck and who knows what—
I earn my daily bread teaching poetry
and appear here as a guest, a former
rancher, a part-time loader of hay.

"What a load of shit," she said again
and this time I asked, "What?"
while imagining the poetry
that might be made from drudgery
and dead-end jobs. She shook her head
in disgust and waved her arms angrily.
In the artificial breeze, the air grew
hotter and the dried grass rattled
like a snake about to strike.

Corn Flakes

We were having breakfast
with my mother's sister Annie,
who turned to me and said,
"A neighbor gave us a magazine
with a poem you'd written about
how when you went to college,
your father had you arrested
as a runaway. Did that happen?"

"Yes," I told her and saw
that while she was resigned
to having a writer in the family,
she remained uncertain as to
whether I might now be offering
fact or fiction. "He called the cops."

She turned to my mother
who was eating corn flakes.
"Did that really happen?"

"Yes."

"Well, what did you do?"

"I didn't do anything.
What could I do?"

"Protest?"

My mother put a spoonful
of corn flakes into her mouth.
You could hear a little click
in her jaw as she began to chew.

Dilemmas of the Angels: Waiting

When the bus pulls up, she waits
while the other passengers disembark
then steps down, the click of her shoes
loud on the empty sidewalk.

Facing the terminal is a faux Tejano
cantina. In winter, the metal louvres
on the heater above the pool table rattle
while behind the bar the bottles shiver.
Now in summer, no matter how hard
the air conditioner whirs, the room's hot.

When she opens the door, a mechanical
parrot squawks "hello" and the patrons
turn to shield their eyes against the light.
She orders a diet Coke and fry bread.
The barmaid, who looks about fifteen,
sticks the fry bread in the microwave
The timer ticks down and at zero
the bell on the oven door rings.

"Hell of a life," the man beside her says.
"Eleven years without a drink. What
difference would it make if I started
again, you know, in the big picture?"
He lifts a Dr Pepper and smiles.
"Feels like I'm waiting for something
only I don't know what. How 'bout you?"

Excusing herself, she steps outside
into a wall of heat. The fry bread
was a bad idea—gave her heartburn.
She sits on a bench in the weak shade

of an ash tree, the pain rising in her chest.
"How 'bout you?" she asks the sky.
"Waiting," he said. Checks her watch.
"You know." Checks again. "For what?"

Submission

I was trying to find the address of *Turning Wheel*,
the journal of socially engaged Buddhism,
not so much to read the articles
as to send them an article of my own.

I looked on the World Wide Web and there
in the middle of the listings—*Turning Wheel*
on Karma,
      on Getting Old,
           on Medical Ethics,
    on Money,   on Food,
        on Sexual Misconduct,
on the Death Penalty,
           on Gay Buddhism,
    on Peace in an Age of War—
was the address of *Turning Wheels*,
the official and award-winning magazine
of the Studebaker Driver's Club, packed
with interesting articles about Studebaker
cars, trucks, and people.
                  Heedless
of my writerly responsibilities, I clicked on the site
and read an article on the Commemorative
1950s Sporty Cars postage stamp set,
a series that included the 1953 Studebaker Starliner.

It made me think of a childhood friend
whose mother drove a Studebaker—
a Silver Hawk or Golden Hawk, 1956—
and who wore sunglasses and a scarf
like a romantic star in a Hollywood film
from before the war. She'd take us to school
and when we got out of the car,
blow her son a kiss, blow me one, too.

I was ten and imagined myself her lover
though I couldn't say what a lover would do
and hadn't asked my friend what had happened
to his father. She never mentioned her husband,
never had a boyfriend at the house, never
went on a date. The article explained
that the Starliner was an automobile designed
with the aerodynamic lines and innovative look
that was favored by American GI's returning
from World War II. I'd often see her driving alone.
She'd smile and wave then shout hello as she went by.

I turned off the computer and sat thinking
of my friend's mother and that GI who never
returned, dressed in his ghostly uniform, taking
one hand off the steering wheel of the Studebaker
and leaning over to kiss his wife, turning around
to wink at two of his buddies drinking beer
in the back seat, his son pressed between them,
the men with their legs smashed up to their chests,
the boy wearing a soldier's cap. Jesus, I thought,
forgetting for a moment that I was a writer and
seeing again my friend's mother, her sunglasses
and scarf, her smile and wave, her shouted hello.

Dilemmas of the Angels: Intention

The angel loves Sundays—coffee and the paper—
but it's hard today. A man says he cannot
support a woman's right to abortion
even if she becomes pregnant after being raped.
Such pregnancies, he explains, are
intended by God.

She puts down her coffee, turns away,
and looks out the window into the silence
of the winter morning—the yard filled with leaves
fallen from the hundred-year-old cottonwood tree,
and the two squirrels darting around the trunk as if life
required no thinking.

Maybe the man's right—all killing is murder
no matter the horror of life's creation. Still, it eats
at her—if the Lord intended the pregnancy, he
intended the rape.

She feels his invisible caress and distant gaze,
hands pulling her gown aside, sometimes roughly.
He must know there can be no product
from their union.

That same Sunday morning, a woman gets up
before her husband and teenage daughters.
She's waited all week for this pleasure—
coffee and the paper. But she's out of milk
so, quick, goes to the store, a corner grocery
like in a movie, run by an old couple
who know her name and the girls' names,
even her husband's. When she forgets
the money, they say, "Don't worry,
you can pay next time."

That's when it happens—the rape. The angel
would intervene, wrestle the rapist away,
but she knows it would do no good.

When the Lord got Mary pregnant
he never knew her. He wanted
a miracle and made the only
kind he could.

The squirrels are still running around the tree,
brains swirling in the emptiness of their heads.
The coffee's as cold as the winter wind
blowing the leaves against the window.
The angel would claw the skin off her bones,
but she has no bones, no parts
anyone can touch.

She shivers, then unbuttons her robe.
Let the Lord watch and imagine
what he intends.

First Communion Dress

Six of us, my sister says—
childhood friends—had dinner together
and decided to burn what we'd been.

It wasn't the wine or our age,
the slow grinding to a halt at the station
in a city we'd never seen, not knowing
the language and being, as usual,
a little short on money.
It was something else—
the butterflies in our stomachs,
the women we'd not become,
tired of old stuff owning us.

The next day we met again.
Though it was spring, a light snow
was falling. We built a fire in the yard.
Miriam burned her Hebrew books—
"Thirty-three years since I looked at them."
She was happy to no longer be a Jew
and happier still to not yet be a Christian

Linda, the prom queen, threw away
her paper crown with the glued-on
glass diamonds, and Amy, who spent
the winter on the slopes, dropped
her skis into the fire.

Then it was my turn. I held up a battered
cardboard box, the corners taped together.
Sometimes I'd take the box down, open it,
and see, flattened and still, the girl I'd been.

The snow let up; the temperature dropped.
I shivered and threw the dress in.

The Phone Rings

That means our mother is on the plane
flying away from my sister,
who doesn't wait for my hello to begin.

When we were children and our father
came after us, she'd hide under the bed.
Too big to crawl after her, he'd lie down
and press his face to the floor, grabbing
with one arm as she backed away.

From the doorway our mother would call
to him. "Art," she'd say, "Art. Stop."
Low like when we recited The Lord's
Prayer—*Our father who art in Heaven*—
and I think, *Please, no art in Heaven.*

"I can't stand it," my sister says. "I asked her
why she didn't protect us and she said she did
the best she could. I said our responsibility
is not to do the best we can. It's to do what must
be done, no matter what. Then I felt terrible."

I know my sister is right but I say nothing,
seeing my mother standing there, hearing her
calling his name, "Art" and again, "Art. Stop."

Housework

I'm on a stepladder, spackling
a crack that opened in the wall
after an earthquake. My father
did this same work. At home,
he hit my mother—how soft
her face was. She told him,
"Never again." When he hit
his children she stayed quiet.

Even in small earthquakes
there are aftershocks and this
one's no different. The ground
shaking again, I climb down
the ladder and sit on the floor.

My father away, my mother made
us sandwiches then gave the silent
blessing. Holding hands, I hoped
she couldn't read my thoughts.
Not that he hit us that often, I mean,
maybe, you know, I'm exaggerating.

I look out the window and watch
the leaves trembling on the trees.

For forty years she grew quieter,
one day whispering that she felt
short of breath, that her breathing
wasn't right, she couldn't breathe.

I get the broom and sweep up
bread crumbs and lint and hair.
I scrub the toilet then attack
the ring in the tub. It's hot
and sweat drips into my eyes.

My mother died without a word
to me nor I to her. Who knows
when the house will stop shaking,
if it's worth spackling the crack.

Dilemmas of the Angels: Prayer

Not that angels ordinarily pray,
but she's been around people
a long time. "Please God, let me . . ."
she starts but it sounds so childish,
a little girl asking permission to be.

"I grant you free will," says the Lord,
playing the role of a genie in a lamp.
"Do me the favor, make the right choice."
Because he's so tall, she has to look up
to see if he's speaking ironically.

Maybe pray to someone else, maybe
a Greek—Aphrodite, Athena, Artemis.
At least they're women. Still, they can be
as vengeful as men, always threatening
to bust up someone's boat and let it sink
to the bottom of someone else's wine-dark
sea. Or is that only the Sirens singing so men
drift into the rocks? Maybe the tricksters—
Spider, Raven, and Coyote—Spider dropping
on silk thread into a woman's underwear,
Raven strutting along the beach then pissing
in the surf, Coyote waving his penis and farting
at presidential parties. At least he's cute and he
never gets any older or pretends to get any wiser.

Say they're all tricksters, God the biggest
of them all. It gives her a headache and an itch
in her body. She flaps her wings and floats
into the sky. Below her there's an ash tree
and a red dirt road, a hill rising above a plain
and a rush of water in a creek, a boy fishing
with a line that has no hook. He has dark hair
and looks like the young Buddha. Another boy,

hiding behind a tree, fires an arrow that strikes
her wing. Crying out, she falls. When she wakes,
it's in a room filled with the scent of cardamom
and smoke. Light streams through the windows.
Someone has cleaned and dressed her wound.
A boy stands beside the bed. She tries to sit up
and the boy points at her wing, the clean bandage
covering the ragged gash where the arrow entered,
the hollow bone and bits of broken feather shaft.
He waggles his head like a trader suggesting
maybe yes, maybe no, then he folds his hands
and she, head falling to the pillow, closes her eyes.

Camping Alone

It's strange to be in the woods, almost old.
I love the sky but when I lie down to sleep,
I admit it's not as comfortable on the hard earth
as on my expensive mattress in town.
Across the border in America,
a blinding light flashes toward the sea

and there I am at the bottom of that sea,
floating in my mother's womb, my older
brother's ear to her stomach, listening to America
in the fifties as it pretends to sleep
after the long war, the broken towns,
and the bodies not yet removed from the earth.

I saved my father's photo album, those unearthly
images of him as a soldier. I'd hoped to see
an ordinary man returning to his hometown,
not a victim of a war still limping in old
age toward its armistice. He wanted to sleep,
to disappear into the distances of America.

Outside I heard shots, the snort of a mare, a caw
from a raven as it ricocheted off the metallic earth.
Even in the country, there's no peace in sleep.
The phone rings in my dreams. I answer, "Sí,
¿Quién es?" forgetting which tongue to use, too old
to switch quickly and aware I am lost in my own town.

Next day, my father pulled up in the Lincoln Town
Car he'd bought new and driven across America—
large as a tank swiveling its gun in the same old
circular pattern. He was uncertain if scorched earth
was the best course of action, or boiling seas,
or if, finally, it was time to go home to sleep.

Now he's dead and each morning I want to sleep
late but I get up, shave, dress, and drive downtown
to an office of computers and copy machines, a sea
of bright technology humming across America.
I wish we were together in the tent, the hard earth
beneath us, no matter our wars, no matter how old.

Sunday Drive

Some days I think of nothing
but angels. It's true I'm getting
older—no spring chicken.

I've seen death more often
now and she's dressed better.
One night I heard her
rapping at my windowpane.
"For Christ's sake!" I shouted.
"There's no need to be melodramatic.
You can come in by the door."

Cindy had a dream in which
I was killed driving my VW Beetle.
It's a diesel that's supposed to get
fifty miles to the gallon but gets
forty-five if I'm lucky.

What more can I do?
It's our petroleum dependency
that heralds the end. "Don't drive
for two weeks," Cindy told me.
"I mean it. I'm scared."

For ten days I raked leaves
into piles and burned them.
I turned over the garden
and drained the hoses.

Now I'm sitting on the deck
wrapped in layers of clothes
and drinking tea, the clouds
of steam rising to heaven.

Dilemmas of the Angels: The Table

The problem is not the table but the man
writing. Dressed in a blue cotton work shirt,
soft from many washings, he looks nice enough.
The angel thinks he must be the author
of this book, but when she asks, he says no
and points off the page.

Dizzy, she asks the man if she might sit down.
"It's possible," he says. "I'll get you a glass of water."

She wonders if he's sure he's not the author
and he explains that he could be but he's busy.
"We must all have our own projects," he says,
"all have a life of our own. The old people
believed that when a person dies, the soul flies
from the body." She looks up and I wave
but she doesn't see.

"Is it true," she asks, "that you don't decide
what to write, that someone else is writing
your words?" "We are predestined," he says,
then, "I don't really believe that. I just had to say it."

Only now does the angel notice how battered
the table is. For years, it was in the kitchen
of our family's hunting camp. Each fall
my grandfather followed deer and elk
through the early snows to their deaths,
butchering the animals on the table,
wrapping the meat to freeze for the winter.
One year he followed them to his own death
and soon enough I will follow them to mine.

"Well, is it true?" the angel asks again.
The man says, "I'm writing a poem."

When I brought the table home, it was black
with years of animal blood and rifle oil.
I sanded the wood but there remained
deep scars from knife cuts and dropped tools—
bone saws and awls. I've never told the man
anything. We all need a certain privacy
and literature is not, after all, the place
where everything is to be revealed.

I'm about to wave again, but as I lift
my arm, she turns and I am blinded by how
really beautiful she is, more beautiful than I
could imagine. Then it strikes me how little
I know about her thoughts and I feel shy,
ashamed of how much I have presumed.

Before I can apologize, the man slides
his chair closer to her and rests his head
on her shoulder. She takes his hand
and they look out the window onto a world
that from this vantage point, I'm unable to see.

In Bed

I'd hoped my wife and I might make love,
but she showed no interest in my hesitant advances
and I was too shy to ask.

I'm reading with a headlamp as if spelunking
toward an underground river or skiing at night,
the moonlight snow rising from the slope.

My wife might change her mind, but for now
she rumbles down the track ahead of me,
a train steaming toward its secret station.

With eternity before us, there's plenty of time
for the embarrassments of aging—flesh pooling
at the waist, liver spots darkening hands and face, hair.

The unknown is as ordinary as socks and our spirits
as transparent as the gown my wife wears in bed,
her body released from the prison of day.

With a snort, she throws an arm across my chest
knocking the book to the floor. I switch off the light,
take a breath, and imagine what comes next.

Falling Asleep

I lie down as if I were a child
and count my blessings—
my mother and father
and how I follow them
on their journey, keeping
a slight distance.

The immortal fragile day—
a small boat on a glassy lake.
I take the sail down
and the boat drifts
in open water far from shore.

CPSIA information can be obtained
at www.ICGtesting.com
Printed in the USA
LVOW10s1342230117

521870LV00001B/89/P